Receptivity

Receptivity

Francis Kelly Nemeck, O.M.I.

VANTAGE PRESS
New York / Washington / Atlanta
Los Angeles / Chicago

Imprimi Potest: Michael Pfeifer, O.M.I.,
Provincial of the Southern United States Province

Imprimatur: + *Thomas J. Drury, Bishop of Corpus Christi, Texas*

To

Christ Jesus:
Yesterday—Today—Forever

in

Loving Memory

of

Francis Leonard "Kelly" Nemeck
(1910–1960)

"I believe that what we suffer in this life
can in no way be compared with the glory which
is awaiting us" (Rom. 8:18).

Contents

Preface

Receptivity is a study of what it means to be receptive to God as found in the spiritual theology of Père Pierre Teilhard de Chardin and compared with certain aspects of the dark night of the soul in St. John of the Cross.

Receptivity is the fundamental and all-pervasive attitude of creature vis-à-vis Creator: What have we—indeed, what are we—that we have not received? (1 Cor. 4:7). Our awareness of the quality of our receptivity attains a particularly acute degree of consciousness in suffering and in praying. Intense suffering and profound prayer are the ordinary milieus in which we experience most unmistakably our inner poverty before God, together with his incomparable love transforming us in himself.

This book then deals with the mystery of suffering and the mystery of praying as they converge deep within us to form our personal response to letting God be done within us. In a sense, therefore, this study views suffering as praying, or at least as a unique potential to pray.

General Notes to the Reader

Note 1. The research which underlies this book began originally as a doctoral study under the direction of Henri Cardinal de Lubac, S.J. Those studies led to a dissertation entitled *Les "passivités" dans la mystique teilhardienne* (1973). This was later co-published by Les Editions Desclée (Paris) and by Les Editions Bellarmin (Montreal) as volume 20 of their series *Hier/Aujourd'hui* under the title *Teilhard de Chardin et Jean de la Croix* (1975). *Receptivity* (1985) represents a completely revised presentation of the original research redacted in the light of subsequent insight and adapted to an English-speaking readership.

Note 2. References to the works of Teilhard are made to English translations whenever possible. References to the writings of St. John of the Cross are made in the usual manner. All translations of either author as well as of biblical passages in this study are my own. I frequently adapt these texts to express contemporary inclusive language.

Note 3. There are two peculiarities notable in Teilhard's literary style: (1) He often capitalizes words which ordinarily would not be capitalized either in French or in English. He does this for emphasis or to give them a special meaning. I have retained this element of his style since it does serve a useful purpose in interpreting certain passages; for example, *le Monde,* the World. (2) Teilhard coins and even "creates" many words and technical expressions particular to himself. Usually I paraphrase these into intelligible English (e.g., *par traversée*, by going all the way through). Sometimes I transliterate them (e.g., *le Christique*, the Christic). Once in a while I retain the French word itself (e.g., *Milieu*, Milieu).

Note 4. Following the Western mystical tradition, both John and Teilhard use the word "soul" (*anima, el alma, l'âme*) as synonymous with "person," stressing the interiority of that person. This usage does not come from the scholastic *corpus-anima distinction*, but rather is derived from the New Testament *psyche* and the Hebrew *nephesh*, which denote the deepest and most mysterious aspects of the human person being acted upon by God. I use the word "soul" in this same sense.

Note 5. Together with Teilhard (and John) I recognize the traditional Christian usage of the term "passivity" to denote our attitude of loving receptivity with regard to the divine transforming and purifying activity within us. Generally, however, I translate *passivité* by "receptivity" (a less equivocal word in English than "passivity"). Teilhard frequently uses the term in the plural (*les passivités*) to refer to a whole complex of events which befall a person: hence, that which we receive, undergo. In these instances I habitually retain the word "passivities."

Note 6. There are two pecularities of my own with regard to the terminology employed in this book: (1) I consistently use the traditional Christian terms "deification" and "divinization" in place of the more current word "sanctification." Deification and divinization denote more explicitly our movement towards transforming union in love with God. (See *Contemplation*, pp. 13–20). And (2) I consistently employ the word "stop" in an unusual way: e.g., the stop of the will on some creature. Within the basic analogy of a pilgrim's journey to God and in him, the term "stop" describes more graphically the effect of attachment to a creature than do some of its synonyms, like "fixation."

Abbreviations

AE	Teilhard de Chardin, Pierre. *Activation of Energy*. New York: Harcourt Brace Jovanovich, Inc., 1970.
Ascent	St. John of the Cross. *The Ascent of Mount Carmel*. Various editions, publications and translations.
Canticle	St. John of the Cross. *The Spiritual Canticle* (second redaction). Various editions, publications and translations.
CE	Teilhard de Chardin, Pierre. *Christianity and Evolution*. New York: Harcourt Brace Jovanovich, Inc., 1971.
Contemplation	Nemeck, Francis Kelly and Coombs, Marie Theresa. *Contemplation*. Wilmington: Michael Glazier, Inc., 1982.
Cor.	Whitman, William, trans. *Pierre Teilhard de Chardin and Maurice Blondel: Correspondence*. New York: Herder and Herder, 1967.
DM	Teilhard de Chardin, Pierre. *The Divine Milieu*. New York: Harper Torchbooks, 1960.
Flame	St. John of the Cross. *The Living Flame of Love* (second redaction). Various editions, publications and translations.
FM	Teilhard de Chardin, Pierre. *The Future of Man*. New York: Harper Torchbooks, 1964.

HE	Teilhard de Chardin, Pierre. *Human Energy.* New York: Harcourt Brace Jovanovich, Inc., 1969.
HM	Teilhard de Chardin, Pierre. *The Heart of Matter.* New York: Harcourt Brace Jovanovich, Inc., 1978.
HU	Teilhard de Chardin, Pierre. *Hymn of the Universe.* New York: Harper and Row, 1965.
Journal	Teilhard de Chardin, Pierre. *Personal Journals: I–XXI, 1915–1955.* Unpublished.
LT	Teilhard de Chardin, Pierre. *Letters from a Traveller.* New York: Harper and Row, 1962.
MM	Teilhard de Chardin, Pierre. *The Making of a Mind.* New York: Harper and Row, 1965.
Night	St. John of the Cross. *The Dark Night of the Soul.* Various editions, publications and translations.
PM	Teilhard de Chardin, Pierre. *The Phenomenon of Man.* New York: Harper Torchbooks, 1961.
SC	Teilhard de Chardin, Pierre. *Science and Christ.* New York: Harper and Row, 1968.
TF	Teilhard de Chardin, Pierre. *Towards the Future.* Harcourt Brace Jovanovich, Inc., 1975.
Writings	Teilhard de Chardin, Pierre. *Writings in Time of War.* New York: Harper and Row, 1968.

Receptivity

Introduction

This book has been a long time in the making. Not that the research which it embodies was all that difficult or drawn out, but rather that its underlying question has persisted in me as far back as I can remember. The philosophers of old refer to this as "the problem of evil." The irreligious express it: "If God is really so good and provident, how do you account for so much pain, injustice and death in the world?" Everyone at one time or another has cried at least in his/her own heart: "Why, Lord? Why must I suffer?" Even the mother of Jesus lamented on a particular occasion: "Son, why have you done this to us?" (Luke 2:48).

From an early age I tended to gravitate toward authors who, in one way or another, addressed this question in a positive and constructive manner. Yet experience proved to be the best teacher. All around me and deep within myself I could see, feel, intuit a great deal of good emanating from suffering, pain, even death. And my faith confirmed it. But how could this be? Why?

The various explanations of this truth offered by the authors I had read left me ultimately unsatisfied. This restlessness in turn forced me to search further and deeper, for my faith and my experience were seeking a better understanding of this mystery.

It was inevitable that one day I should come across the writings of St. John of the Cross (1542–1591). No one has ever succeeded in putting the dark night of the soul in more positive light than the Mystical Doctor himself. It was about this time also that I stumbled upon some essays on this general subject by

Pierre Teilhard de Chardin (1881–1955). In an instant I knew the definitive direction in which the rest of this quest would take me. In the combined insights of these two great men we have one of the most profound and far-reaching approaches to the mystery of receptivity—our innermost attitude towards God in all that we must undergo—that has ever been written. What remained, however, was for someone to bring together the insights of these two masters.

Thus was conceived the search (and the research) which, after much pain and contradiction, after many setbacks and rejections, after even several deaths and peregrinations across two continents, finally gave birth to this book. So, if at first sight this study looks like a scholarly work, please know that the context of its composition and its real purpose far transcend any purely academic endeavor. This work is truly the fruit of a persistent and deeply personal quest which came to pose itself in these terms: What could possibly be the positive and perfective value of all that we must undergo throughout life—especially of all that we must suffer and die to?

1. The Scope of this Study

Among the recent thinkers who have tried to fathom the mystery of receptivity one would certainly have to recognize the contribution of Père Teilhard. Works on this eminent French scientist and mystic are numerous and varied. Yet to date no one has attempted a comprehensive study of his insights on the many dimensions of this mystery. A number of treatises on various aspects of his spirituality do exist, yet not one tries to synthesize and evaluate the full extent of Teilhard's teaching concerning the role of receptivity in our divinization.

Most knowledgeable people would quite readily associate the name of Teilhard with activity: an active or apostolic spirituality. In effect, one still occasionally runs across the criticism that "de Chardin" (as many English-speaking persons mistakenly refer to him) is too activity-oriented, foolishly optimistic or downright naive about building up the Body of Christ. In reality, however, he never lost sight of the primacy of receptivity, not only in the spiritual life, but also in all life. For even as a young man Teilhard readily admitted how essential are *les passivités:* "In spite of the fundamental importance I have always tended to give human effort and development, I recognize that the soul does not even begin to know God until it has really had to suffer diminishment in him. So, abandon yourself to our Lord. Let yourself be swept along by him."[1]

The principal subject of this study is, therefore, an aspect of Teilhard's spirituality. But we shall also be comparing this aspect to its counterpart in the mystical theology of St. John of the Cross. The reason for this comparison is twofold. First of all, Teilhard himself suggests its importance. Yet even had he not so indicated, such a comparison would still be necessary in order to authenticate the veracity of his spiritual insights with respect to the teaching of the Mystical Doctor of the Church.

A. Reflections by Teilhard on John of the Cross

One would hardly consider the co-reformer of Carmel a spiritual mentor of Teilhard, since his references to John are comparatively few and far between. Nevertheless, they do extend over a period of thirty-two years and have a bearing on his interior development. We shall group these remarks chronologically: (1) after World War I; (2) after the composition of *The Divine Milieu* (1927); and (3) after World War II.

(1) After World War I

In an entry of his *Journal* dated December 22, 1923, Teilhard opposes what he remembers having read of John of the Cross back in 1917: "They [John and others] look upon the World as unnourishing and so conclude that God must give himself in complete substitution for it." God wipes it out, as it were. "Let us close our windows on the World and the divine light will shine within us." Teilhard then goes on to present his own position: "God gives himself to us by *assimilation* of the Real (by shining through, by sublimation, by a certain 'transubstantiation'). God illumines by way of synthesis—beyond light. . . . This latter solution is based on a profound metaphysics of Being and of Love."

Since Teilhard's knowledge of Spanish was quite limited, he could not have read John in the original Castilian. Did Teilhard then encounter John in some nineteenth-century French translation, or did he merely read about him in some unidentified, possibly even Jansenistic, commentator? We do not know. What is apparent, however, is that Teilhard appreciated some and misunderstood other key notions of the co-reformer of Carmel.

Teilhard indicates for the first time what he understands by "nights" in a paragraph written shortly after his "retreat of demobilization."[2] In this reflection he interprets well what John means by the purification of the soul: "*The nights* (deaths). In order to attain the Universal Element (Christ) hidden in the innermost being of all creatures, we must not only complete them, but we must also pass all the way through them as if through a series of successive layers. This passing through. . . . is a detachment, a night, a death." He continues: "As we arrive at each successive layer, we find that it is all resplendent with the Divine Presence abiding deep within it. But later, after we have advanced further, we discover that the Divine is no longer in that zone *for us* (it has become obscure). We must then be detached. For it is by means of successive attachments and detachments that God emerges *for us*" from within us.

Let us note two details couched in these texts (details which differentiate Teilhard from John of the Cross). First, Teilhard insists not only on detachment from and renunciation of the stop

4

of the will on a creature, but also upon the *completion* and the *use* of the created being as necessary to the mystical life. Second, Teilhard does not ordinarily employ the expression "dark nights." He prefers rather the symbol of a Presence so diffuse or of a Synthesis so simple that it is impossible to know them adequately or to express them clearly.[3] In other words, Teilhard tends to accentuate the positive and constructive aspects of all created beings, and therefore has difficulty with John's explanation of the dark night of the soul as he understood it: namely, as being supposedly devoid of completion and use, depleted of Presence and Synthesis.

In a paper drafted for Maurice Blondel in December 1919, Teilhard criticizes in passing an ascetical attitude which he attributes to the co-reformer of Carmel: This "form of *renunciation* is that of a *cutting off,* a *rupture* with the world, an *evacuation* pure and simple of the old man. St. John of the Cross understood literally seems to conceive of the Night in just that way. Do you want to find God? Then close the avenues which let in the false exterior life. Once you have done this, *ipso facto* the higher light will appear, while the other one vanishes. The exterior noise having ceased, you hear the other voice in your heart. For there are *two* entirely distinct lights illuminating you. There are two different words reverberating continually within you. To discern the one properly you must extinguish the other. The new Earth. . . . succeeds the old Earth by pushing it aside and taking its place."[4]

Thus, prior to 1926, when St. John of the Cross was proclaimed Doctor of the universal Church in all matters ascetical and mystical, Teilhard's attitude towards his doctrine of the night can be summarized in these four points:

(1) Teilhard searched into the reality which John calls the "dark night," and (2) he perceived quite well its underlying mystery. But (3) he vigorously reacted against a form of renunciation

that he believed he saw in the literal sense of certain Sanjuanist texts, without however (4) rejecting what we may term the spirit of the mystical night. "Detachment and human effort do harmonize," Teilhard insists. "Moreover, there is no limit to their variety and combination. Vocations are limitless and in each life one finds an infinity of phases. There is within the Church St. Thomas Aquinas and St. Vincent de Paul side by side with St. John of the Cross."[5]

(2) After the Composition of The Divine Milieu (1927)

In a brief but important essay entitled *The Road of the West: Towards a New Mysticism* (1932), Teilhard observes the following: "It appears that the mystical history of the West can be described as a lengthy endeavor by Christianity to recognize and separate within itself the two fundamental ways of spiritualization: the Eastern and the Western. That is, respectively: *suppression* and *sublimation*. . . . Many have tried to find in this duality two essential and compatible constituents of holiness. But they are in reality nothing more than the vestige of two irreconcilable attitudes. Carried along and corrected by the general movement of Christianity, persons like St. John of the Cross have undoubtedly lived in actual fact a mysticism reducible to that of the sublimation of creatures and their convergence in God. But the manner in which they have expressed themselves (or at least the way others have interpreted the expression of their experience) is still decidedly 'Eastern.' "

By "Eastern" Teilhard means an approach to mysticism which accentuates suppression, withdrawal from the World, negation of creatures: in other words, the opposite of a mysticism based on love, union and transformation.[6] Teilhard concludes his thought with this observation: "We must have the honesty to recognize that in this aspect of their sanctity they are no longer meaningful to us."[7]

In the above passage Teilhard does acknowledge that John is a most authentic model of Christian mysticism, at least in the way in which he lived. However, certain expressions used by John in his writings to describe his personal mystical experience, together with the interpretations given by some of his commentators, leave the impression—according to Teilhard—of a doctrine irreconcilable with that of the sublimation of creatures and their convergence in God.

If such were indeed the case, then we would have to agree that at least that aspect of the Mystical Doctor is no longer appropriate for our times. However, beyond the appearances of certain passages, is not the role of creatures in our divinization—*explicit* doctrine in the writings of John—radically positive, dynamic and unitive? We shall see that it is so.

(3) After World War II

Between 1945 and 1951 Teilhard's thoughts return several times to the co-reformer of Carmel.

On August 25, 1945, in an entry in his *Journal,* he poses this question (without, however, giving himself a response): "A case of 'complementarity'. . . . the mystical passivity of a John of the Cross?"—the complement being, according to the context, his own theology of receptivity.

In a major essay entitled *My Fundamental Vision* (1948), Teilhard twice and without qualification designates St. John of the Cross as a model of the very mysticism of loving union and transformation which he himself teaches.[8] This mysticism is clearly that which he terms "the Road of the West."

On February 1, 1950, in his *Journal,* Teilhard deals schematically with the Sanjuanist term *nada* in a context which treats of the mystical act of love.

On January 15, 1951, again in his *Journal,* he poses this question (once more without giving a response): "Is a 'night' necessary prior to the mysticism of 'passing all the way through'?"

Finally, in *Some Notes on the Mystical Sense* (1951), Teilhard attempts to clarify an obscure paragraph in an earlier essay in which he had mentioned John of the Cross.[9] His clarification reads: "Both in theory and in practice Christianity not only follows, but *is* the Road of the West. Yet, we must recognize that. . . the Judeo-Christian mystical current has had some difficulty in breaking away from a perspective which has sought *Oneness* too exclusively in *Separateness* rather than in the *Unifying and Transforming Power* of God. God *over and above* all things (rather than God *in* and *through* all things). This attitude brings about a veritable 'impoverishment' of our mystical theology. . . for it is not sufficiently universal and cosmic. There are, however, some notable exceptions: Eckhart, Francis of Assisi, St. John of the Cross."[10]

Teilhard's views and questions concerning the Mystical Doctor can be reduced to these six: (1) He grasps well the essence of the mystery which John calls "night." Yet, (2) Teilhard criticizes the letter—the actual verbal expression—of the Sanjuanist doctrine of purification, which he considers static and too negative. Nevertheless, (3) he does recognize in John's lived experience a model of that mysticism which has at its core the sublimation of creatures and their convergence in God, although he does not perceive these same qualities in John's writings. However, (4) towards the end of his life, Teilhard does not hesitate to consider without qualification St. John of the Cross as equal to St. Francis of Assisi in that which pertains to an authentic Christian love of creatures. (5) As for loving union with God, he wholeheartedly recognizes the unique contribution of John to the understanding of Western mystical theology. Finally, (6) Teilhard is led one day to question himself concerning the possible complementarity of his own conviction regarding receptivity to God in comparison to the mystical passivity of St. John of the Cross.

Teilhard's attitude towards John underwent a gradual development without, however, any significant change of view.

8

Although he saw in the Sanjuanist mysticism of transforming union an exemplary formulation of the Christian mystery, Teilhard still never felt completely at ease with John's manner of expressing the theology of purification. Moreover, Teilhard clearly wished to make his own contribution to the Church's mystical tradition—a contribution not only in comparison to the co-reformer of Carmel, but also in relation to all the spiritual masters who had preceded him on the Road of the West. That is, he attempted to contribute by means of complementarity, trying to focus explicitly on certain aspects of this mystical tradition which up to his time at least had far too long remained in the background.

B. Three Questions Examined in this Study

Among Teilhard's comments on John of the Cross, two criticisms merit special consideration: (1) Teilhard viewed John's theology of the role of creatures in our interior progress as neither positive in itself nor relevant to our times. (2) John's manner of expressing the reality of the night appeared to Teilhard static and too negative. A first question we shall take up, therefore, is this: What actually is the role of creatures in our sanctification, and how does the purifying process produce unifying results according to the Mystical Doctor?

Teilhard himself considers John of the Cross a necessary point of reference for any authentic mysticism. Thus, he is aware of the importance of John's doctrine as a standard for comparison with his own. Now, if Teilhard's teaching on passive purification is truly Christian, there must then be points of convergence between the two mystics. A second question is this: What then is the core of his theology concerning receptivity, and does convergence indeed exist between John and Teilhard on this subject?

A third question may be posed this way: Has Teilhard made a personal contribution to the understanding of the mystery of Christian receptivity?

Thus, our immediate concern in this book is to study what it means to be receptive to God in the mystical theology of Teilhard. The corresponding doctrine in the writings of St. John of the Cross is set forth for two reasons: *on the one hand,* to explore the possibility of finding on his teachings of the night something other than "cutting off, rupture with the World, evacuation pure and simple of the old man." And *on the other hand,* the Mystical Doctor will serve as a necessary point of reference for authenticating Teilhard's own teaching on receptivity.

Our ultimate concern in this book, however, is this: that, having studied receptivity in John and in Teilhard and having compared their respective insights, we ourselves may come to a heightened appreciation of this mystery so essential to true growth in Christ and so integral to loving union with God.

2. The Outline of this Study

Our research unfolds in three phases: (1) John of the Cross, (2) Teilhard de Chardin, (3) divergence between and convergence of the two mystics.

The basic movement underlying these three phases is that of a dialectic. Whether the expression is "the Ascent of Mount Carmel" or "the Law of Complexity-Consciousness," in both instances a dynamic process is at work. The intricacies of the theories of evolution certainly never occurred to John of the Cross. Nonetheless, he truly lived and gave expression to the profound dynamics latent within his Christian faith. As for Teilhard, did not the core of his originality even in the scientific realm proceed also from his profound Christian commitment?

The faith life of the Church is not only in evolution, it is especially in *genesis.*[11] Indeed, it is in *Christogenesis.*[12] Over the centuries, long before Darwin or Huxley, true Christian mystics had been spontaneously swept along by a movement emanating from deep within the Gospel. This movement ascends relentlessly towards the Parousia. The dynamism of Christ has always been at the very soul of Christian mysticism, with the person of Jesus its Way, its Alpha and its Omega. The various components of a genesis can be viewed chronologically and divided into past, present and future. Or they can be discerned more profoundly in the phases of their dialectic movement so as to be distinguished in their divergence and convergence. I have chosen the latter approach, from which emerges the outline found in the table of contents.

Notes from Introduction

1. *MM*, Jan. 11, 1919, p. 275.
2. *Journal*, Mar. 31, 1919. His retreat was March 16–23 near Lyons.
3. See *Writings*, pp. 70-71, 117-149; *HU*, pp. 19-37, 41-55, 59-71; *DM*, pp. 112-149; *HM*, pp. 39–58, 61–77, 82–102.
4. *Cor.*, p. 31.
5. *Cor.*, p. 35.
6. See *TF*, pp. 40–59, 101–106, 134–147, 199–205, 209–211.
7. *TF*, pp. 51–52.
8. *TF*, pp. 194 (note 30) and 201.
9. The essay is: "Two Converse Forms of Spirit" (1950), in *AE*, p. 225.
10. *TF*, pp. 210–211. Teilhard's insistence on the immanence of God (ie., attaining him *en et à travers toutes choses*) in no way diminishes his conviction of the absolute transcendence of God (ie., the fact that he remains always infinitely distinct from, superior to and *au-delà* his creation). See *AE*, pp. 97–127, 215–227; *CE*, pp. 56–95; *HM*, 15–16, 39–58.
11. "Confusion often exists between what is called 'evolution' and what is called 'genesis.' Evolution can be directionless, periodic, in any-which-way (at least in theory). . . . But genesis is evolution directed towards a point of consummation" (Teilhard, letter to Fr. Fleming, May 19, 1954).
12. In the actual economy of salvation the point of ultimate consummation is the person of Jesus Christ. See *HM*, pp. 82–102; *CE*, pp. 76–95, 237–245; *TF*, pp. 212–215.

Phase I

St. John of the Cross

Preliminary Remarks

An initial perusal of the works of the Mystical Doctor can easily shock the uninformed reader. Take, for example, these sentiments expressed in the *Ascent of Mount Carmel.*

In order to mortify and put to rest our "natural passions" we must first "seek always to be inclined":

Not to the easiest, but to the most difficult.
Not to the most delightful, but to the most distasteful. . . .
Not to the most, but to the least. . . .
Seek not the best of temporal things, but the worst. . . .
Desire to enter into complete detachment, emptiness and poverty
   with respect to everything in the world [for the sake of Christ].

Diligent practice of the above may suffice to enter into the night of sense. But if you honestly wish to intensify the action of grace within yourself, much more is required:

Try to act with contempt for yourself, and desire that all others
   do the same. . . .
Endeavor to speak disparagingly of yourself, and desire that all
   others do likewise. . . .
Seek to have a lowly opinion of yourself, and desire that all others
   have the same.[2]

And, as if that were not enough:

To reach enjoyment in all, strive to enjoy nothing. . . .
To arrive at being all, will to be nothing. . . .

15

For to pass from all to all, you must be stripped of all in all.

And when you possess all, you must do so without desiring anything. . . .

Only in this nakedness does the spiritual soul find its peace and repose. Since it covets nothing, nothing fatigues it in straining forward, and nothing causes it to close in upon itself.[3]

From an initial exposure to such texts a barrage of questions surges: Is not this way of *nada* more narrow than the Sermon on the Mount? Are not these expressions but typical Mediterranean exaggerations—hyperboles peculiar to the Castilian temperament? How can one who takes them literally avoid suffering for the sake of suffering? Must we not at least recognize that this Sanjuanist asceticism pertains to a vocation so rare, so unique, that it is for all practical purposes extinct?

An adequate response to these questions would surely require more than two brief chapters. So, rather than attempt a direct answer, I shall synthesize the gist of these sayings of John to see what bearing they have on this study.

The expression of the first two series of statements is obviously quite negative. The third series on the other hand accentuates the dialectic between *todo* and *nada*. This dialectic situates the negative aspect in relation to the positive thrust which dominates the entire purifying process. That is, in the Sanjuanist perspective deification is accomplished by means of a dialectic, the negative aspect of which can be explained only by its radically positive source and goal.

Before studying in more detail the process of this purification (in chapter 2) let us first examine creation as the milieu in which and through which this dynamic operates (chapter1).

Notes from Preliminary Remarks

1. *Ascent,* I, 13, 6.
2. *Ascent,* I, 13, 9.
3. *Ascent,* I, 13, 11.